City Shapes

Triangles

By Jennifer S. Burke

Welcome Books

Children's Press
A Division of Grolier Publishing
New York / London / Hong Kong / Sydney
Danbury, Connecticut

Photo Credits: Cover, p. 7, 9, 11, 13, 15, 17, 21 © Indexstock; p. 5, 19, 21 by Thaddeus Harden
Contributing Editors: Mark Beyer and Eliza Berkowitz
Book Design: Michael DeLisio

Visit Children's Press on the Internet at:
http://publishing.grolier.com

Library of Congress Cataloging-in-Publication Data

Burke, Jennifer S.
   Triangles / by Jennifer S. Burke.
     p. cm. — (City shapes)
   Includes bibliographical references and index.
   Summary: Simple text and photographs reveal different triangles that can be found in
the city.
   ISBN 0-516-23080-8 (lib. bdg.) — ISBN 0-516-23005-0 (pbk.)
   1. Triangle—Juvenile literature. [1. Triangle.] I. Title. II. Series.

QA482.B93 2000   5697
516'.15—dc21
                                                                              00-027946

Contents

There are many **shapes** in the city.

Sometimes shapes are easy to find.

How many **triangles** do you see in this post?

5

The tops of buildings have different shapes in the city.

Which building tops look like triangles?

While you walk in the city, you can look for triangle shapes.

Some parts of buildings are shaped like triangles.

Which part of this building has a triangle shape?

You can look for triangle shapes in the park.

This fence has many triangles.

How many triangles do you see?

The **Statue** of Liberty has triangles around her **crown**.

How many triangles does she have around her crown?

13

At night you can see this triangle shine.

The lights go on at night. The top of this building is in the shape of a triangle.

15

Some buildings have a triangle shape that reaches up high.

This is a tall building.

The top of the triangle comes to a point.

Sometimes triangle shapes are hard to find.

This triangle was found behind the bench.

The bars hold the bench together.

Triangles can be short, tall, wide, and skinny.

Cities are great places to find triangles.

21

New Words

crown (**krown**) something worn
   on the head by a king or queen
shapes (**shaypz**) the ways things
   look
statue (**stach**-oo) a model of a
   person or thing
triangles (**treye**-an-gulz) shapes
   with three sides

To Find Out More

Books
Pancakes, Crackers, and Pizza: A Book of Shapes
by Marjorie Eberts and Margaret Gisler
Children's Press

Triangles and Pyramids
by Sally Morgan
Raintree Steck-Vaughn Publishers

Triangle, Square, Circle
by William Wegman
Hyperion Books for Children

Index

About the Author
Jennifer S. Burke is a teacher and a writer living in New York City. She holds a master's degree in reading education from Queens College, New York.

Reading Consultants

Kris Flynn, Coordinator, Small School District Literacy, The San Diego County Office of Education

Shelly Forys, Certified Reading Recovery Specialist, W.J. Zahnow Elementary School, Waterloo, IL

Peggy McNamara, Professor, Bank Street College of Education, Reading and Literacy Program